Great Women in U.S. History

by Megan Litwin
illustrated by Aleksey Ivanov

Scott Foresman
is an imprint of

Glenview, Illinois • Boston, Massachusetts • Chandler, Arizona
Upper Saddle River, New Jersey

Every effort has been made to secure permission and provide appropriate credit for photographic material. The publisher deeply regrets any omission and pledges to correct errors called to its attention in subsequent editions.

Unless otherwise acknowledged, all photographs are the property of Scott Foresman, a division of Pearson Education.

ISBN 13: 978-0-328-51408-3
ISBN 10:   0-328-51408-x

10 11 12 13 V0FL 16 15 14

Many years ago, women could not vote, go to college, or hold a well-paying job. Women had to fight against tremendous odds to win those rights. Today, women can go to college, vote, and work at any job they please. Let's look at three remarkable women who made a difference in U.S. history: Babe Didrikson Zaharias, Amelia Earhart, and Eleanor Roosevelt.

Many years ago, women could not go to college. Today, women can achieve almost anything they want.

Babe Didrikson Zaharias

Babe Didrikson Zaharias was born in Texas in 1911. Her real name was Mildred Ella Didrikson, but the neighborhood kids called her "Babe" because she could hit a baseball as well as Babe Ruth.

Babe loved baseball. She didn't care that people told her it was a boy's game. She knew she was just as strong as any boy.

Even as a child, Babe Didrikson Zaharias was a strong batter and a terrific athlete.

It didn't take Babe long to prove she was good at other sports too. In high school, Babe was a star on the basketball team. In 1930, Babe was named an All-American. That meant she was one of the best players in the country.

Babe wanted to succeed at other sports as well. She loved to run the hurdles because it reminded her of running and jumping over the hedges when she was a child. Babe was so good at track-and-field events that the newspapers called her "Texas Tornado." She set records at track meets.

Babe played basketball in high school.

In 1932, Babe went to the Olympic Games in Los Angeles. She set a world record in the javelin throw. A javelin is a type of spear. She won a gold **medal.**

Next, Babe took up golfing. Her golf **strokes** were so strong that she became a champion at that too. In 1950, she was named the Outstanding Woman Athlete of the Half-Century. She died of cancer at a young age, but her memory and courage will live forever.

Babe won an Olympic Gold Medal in the javelin throw.

Amelia Earhart

Amelia Earhart was a famous airplane pilot. But she was even more famous for her sense of adventure. She would not take "no" for an answer. She was born on July 24, 1897, in Kansas. Like Babe, Amelia was a tomboy.

Most people didn't think that women should fly planes. Amelia decided to learn to fly anyway. She worked many jobs to pay for her flying lessons. In 1922, her family helped her buy her first plane. Amelia received her pilot's license in 1923.

Amelia's first plane, *Canary*, was canary yellow.

One day in 1928, Amelia was asked to take part in a dangerous flight. A male pilot and his navigator were flying a plane called *Friendship* across the Atlantic Ocean. Amelia joined them. She became the first woman to fly across the Atlantic.

In 1932, she became even more famous when she flew a plane across the Atlantic by herself. "Can she bake a cake?" the French newspapers asked. Amelia knew she could do that and so much more.

Crowds cheered Amelia's spirit and bravery.

Amelia wanted to fly along the equator and circle the entire Earth. It was very risky. No woman had ever done that before! But Amelia had spirit.

Amelia finished two-thirds of the flight. Then, on July 3, 1937, something went wrong. Amelia and her plane disappeared. No one knows for sure what happened. Maybe her plane ran out of fuel, or maybe she **drowned.** We do know that Ameila Earhart proved that women can do daring things.

Planes searched for Amelia, but she and her plane have never been found.

Eleanor Roosevelt

Eleanor Roosevelt was born on October 11, 1884, in New York City. She grew up in a wealthy family, but money didn't cure her loneliness. It wasn't until Eleanor went to boarding school that she began to see how helping others could make her happy. That was a lesson Eleanor would try to teach others all her life. In 1905, Eleanor married Franklin D. Roosevelt.

As a child, Eleanor learned that she loved helping others.

Then, in 1921, Franklin was stricken with polio. Eleanor became his nurse, but she was much more than that. She began to travel to political meetings for her husband. She saw many injustices and spoke out against them.

Franklin was elected President of the United States in 1932. Eleanor became First Lady. She began to study **current** events. The 1930s was the time of the Great Depression in the United States. Many people had no work or money for food.

When Franklin could no longer walk, Eleanor began to travel for him.

Eleanor traveled across the country and **stirred** hope in the hearts of millions of people. Her motto was "Tomorrow is now." Eleanor helped the poor, and she spoke out for the rights of women and other minorities. She told people, "Do what you feel in your heart to be right."

Even after her husband's death, Eleanor **continued** her work. She fought for human rights and worked for peace. When she died on November 7, 1962, she was one of the most important and beloved women of her time.

Eleanor Roosevelt gave many speeches across the country.

Babe Didrikson Zaharias, Amelia Earhart, and Eleanor Roosevelt were three great women in U.S. history. They worked hard to gain respect for all women. Their determination and bravery led them to do things no one had done before. Every one of us can **celebrate** their successes. Each of us can learn from their courage and spirit.

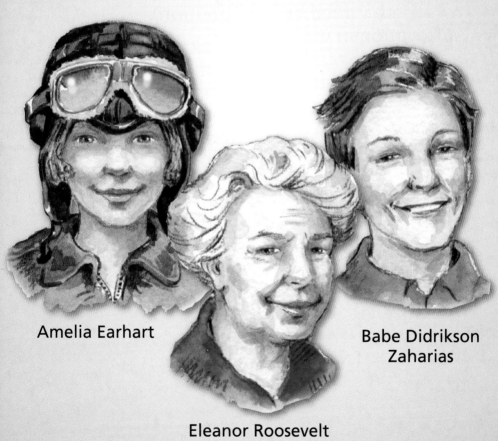

Amelia Earhart

Babe Didrikson Zaharias

Eleanor Roosevelt

Glossary

celebrate *v.* to honor or praise.

continued *v.* went on in some action; kept on.

current *adj.* belonging to the present; in progress.

drowned *v.* died by suffocation in water.

medal *n.* a small piece of metal, usually with a special design, given as an award for some outstanding act.

stirred *v.* awakened or brought to the surface (as in an emotion).

strokes *n.* in tennis, golf, or other ball sports, the motion of striking or hitting the ball.